Magic Bullet Smoothie Recipe Book

Table of Content

IMMUNE SYSTEM SMOOTHIES

INTRODUCTION:

Welcome to the "Magic Bullet Smoothie Recipe Book" – your guide to creating delicious and healthy smoothies with your Magic Bullet Blender for 1500 days. This book is a collection of recipes that are quick, easy to make, and packed with benefits like weight loss, detoxification, disease fighting, energy boosting, and longevity.

The author of this book is a smoothie lover who has spent years gathering and perfecting recipes that can be made in minutes using the Magic Bullet Blender. These recipes are designed to fit into your busy lifestyle while providing all the nutrients you need to stay healthy and energized.

Inside this book, you'll find chapters dedicated to:

- Green Smoothie: Recipes full of leafy greens that boost your energy and vitality.
- Fruit Smoothie: Sweet and refreshing smoothies made from a variety of fruits.
- Vegetable Smoothie: Nutrient-rich smoothies that make vegetables delicious and easy to consume.
- Detox Smoothie: Cleanse your body with smoothies that help eliminate toxins.
- Energy Boost Smoothie: Get an instant energy lift with these revitalizing smoothies.
- Protein Smoothies: Support muscle repair and growth with protein-filled smoothies.
- Immune System Smoothies: Strengthen your immune system with these health-boosting smoothies.
- Weight Loss Smoothie: Aid your weight loss journey with smoothies designed to help you lose weight.
- Blood Sugar-friendly Smoothies: Keep your blood sugar levels steady with these carefully crafted smoothies.
- Kids Friendly Smoothies: Fun and healthy smoothie recipes that kids will love.

You will also learn about the benefits of using the Magic Bullet Blender and how it makes preparing these smoothies a breeze. Its compact size, ease of use, and versatility make it an essential tool in your kitchen for creating healthy meals quickly.

By incorporating these smoothie recipes into your daily routine, you can enjoy the health benefits they offer while also enjoying the process of making them. This book is designed to help you live a healthier life by taking advantage of the convenience and efficiency of the Magic Bullet Blender.

Let this book be your guide to a healthier lifestyle through the power of smoothies. Get ready to transform your health one smoothie at a time.

OVERVIEW OF THE MAGIC BULLET BLENDER:

The Magic Bullet Blender is a compact and versatile blending system designed for personal use. It consists of a high-torque power base and a specially designed blending cup with cross-blade technology. The blender is known for its ability to efficiently blend, grind, and chop a variety of ingredients, making it ideal for creating smoothies, shakes, sauces, dips, and even grinding coffee beans or spices.

One of the key features of the Magic Bullet Blender is its convenience and ease of use. The blending cups are designed to be used for both blending and drinking, eliminating the need for an additional container. The cups have lids and lip rings, making it easy to blend and take your drinks on the go.

Despite its compact size, the Magic Bullet Blender packs a punch with its powerful motor and patented stainless steel cross blades. It can easily pulverize tough ingredients like ice, frozen fruit, and leafy greens, making it a versatile tool for creating healthy and delicious blended drinks.

The Magic Bullet Blender also comes with a variety of accessories, such as additional blending cups, mugs, and a recipe book, to help users explore different blending options and expand their culinary creativity.

BENEFITS OF USING MAGIC BULLET BLENDER

Here are some key benefits of using the Magic Bullet Blender:

- Compact and Space-Saving: The Magic Bullet Blender has a small footprint, making it ideal for small kitchens, countertops, or even dorm rooms. Its compact design allows for easy storage when not in use.
- Versatility: Despite its size, the Magic Bullet can handle a variety of tasks, including blending smoothies, shakes, sauces, dips, and even grinding spices or coffee beans. Its powerful blades can pulverize tough ingredients like ice, frozen fruits, and leafy greens.
- Convenience: The blending cups are designed to be used for both blending and drinking, eliminating the need for an additional container. The cups also come with lids and lip rings, making it easy to take your drinks on the go.
- Time-Saving: The Magic Bullet Blender is designed for personal use, allowing you to quickly blend single or double servings of your favorite drinks or sauces without the hassle of a large blender.
- Easy Cleaning: The blending cups and components are dishwasher-safe, making clean-up a breeze.
- Healthy Choices: With the Magic Bullet, you can easily create nutritious smoothies, protein shakes, and other healthy blended drinks right at home, encouraging a healthier lifestyle.
- Versatile Accessories: The Magic Bullet comes with a variety of accessories, such as additional blending cups, mugs, and a recipe book, allowing you to explore different blending options and expand your culinary creativity.

Overall, the Magic Bullet Blender offers a convenient, compact, and versatile solution for personal blending needs, making it an excellent choice for those with limited kitchen space or those looking for a quick and easy way to incorporate more healthy, blended drinks into their diet.

1. ALL GREEN SMOOTHIE

Total Time: 11 Minutes | Serving: 3

Ingredients

- 1 small avocado, pitted, peeled
- ½ Bartlett pear, seeded
- ½ cup of water
- ½ cup of broccoli florets
- 1 slice pineapple, peeled, with core
- 1 cup of fresh spinach
- 2½ cup of ice cubes
- 3 cups of green grapes

Instructions

1. Put the ingredients in the Magic Bullet blender in order, then close the lid.
2. Set the Magic Bullet blender to its slowest speed initially, then quickly raise it to its fastest setting.
3. For 50 seconds, use the tamper to push the ingredients toward the blades while you blend.

2. BROCCOLI SMOOTHIE

Total Time: 5 Minutes | Serving: 2

Ingredients

- 1 banana (room temperature)
- 1 cup of chopped small broccoli florets
- 1 cup of frozen pineapple chunks
- 1 large green apple, chopped
- ½ cup of water
- ½ cup of Greek yogurt

Instructions

1. Put everything into the Magic Bullet blender. Start by adding the liquids and then the solids. Break up the banana into pieces. Mix until it's smooth. You can eat it right away or put it in the fridge for up to one day in a covered jar.

3. AVOCADO BANANA SMOOTHIE

Total Time: 5 Minutes | Serving: 2

Ingredients

- 1 small ripe banana
- handful of ice
- ½ medium avocado
- 1 cup of almond milk (or regular milk)
- Honey or maple syrup adjusts to your taste
- pistachios for garnish (optional)

Instructions

1. Put everything into a magic bullet blender and blend it until it's smooth.
2. Add pistachios as a garnish and serve right away.

4. BANANA RASPBERRY GREEN SMOOTHIE

Total Time: 10 Minutes | Serving: 4

Ingredients

- 2 cups of almond milk
- 3 cups of frozen raspberries
- 4 small bananas, peeled
- 1 cup of romaine lettuce
- 1/2 cup of fresh mint leaves
- 2 cups of fresh spinach

Instructions

1. Put the ingredients in the Magic Bullet blender in the order given, and then screw the lid on tight.
2. Set the Magic Bullet blender to its slowest speed initially, then quickly raise it to its fastest setting.
3. Using the tamper to push the ingredients toward the blades, blend for 45 seconds or until your desired consistency is reached.

5. SPINACH SMOOTHIE

Total Time: 5 Minutes | Serving: 2

Ingredients

- 10 ice cubes
- ¼ cup of raw cashews
- 1 large green apple
- 4 cups of baby spinach leaves or chopped spinach, loosely packed
- 1 tbsp pure maple syrup
- 1 ½ tbsp fresh squeezed lemon juice (1/2 lemon)
- ½ cup of water

Instructions

1. Apple should be cut into chunks, but the peel should stay on. Put everything into a Magic Bullet blender and blend until smooth. If necessary, stop and scrape the sides of the blender. Try adding the frozen fruit in two parts and blending in between if you choose the fruit option.

6. CELERY SMOOTHIE

Total Time: 5 Minutes | Serving: 2

Ingredients

- 4 medium ribs celery (¾ cup of chopped)
- ½ tsp peeled and grated ginger (from fresh ginger root)
- ½ cup of water
- 2 cups of baby spinach leaves
- 1 ½ tbsp fresh squeezed lemon juice (1/2 lemon)
- 1 large green apple
- 10 ice cubes
- 1 banana

Instructions

1. Make big chunks of the celery. Leave the peel on the apple and cut it into chunks. Cut the banana up. To make ginger, peel it and grate or mince it.
2. Using a magic bullet blender, blend everything until it's smooth. If it's too thick, add a little more water and stop to scrape the sides. It can be drunk right away or kept for up to a day.

7. STRAWBERRY-BANANA GREEN SMOOTHIE

Total Time: 5 Minutes | Serving: 1

Ingredients

- 1 tbsp flaxseeds
- 1 cup of baby spinach
- 1 medium banana
- ½ cup of low-fat plain Greek yogurt
- 6 frozen strawberries
- ½ cup of nonfat milk

Instructions

1. Blend the flaxseeds, yogurt, spinach, strawberries, and bananas using a magic bullet blender until the mixture is smooth.

8. AVOCADO SMOOTHIE

Total Time: 5 Minutes | Serving: 2

Ingredients

- 1/2 ripe avocado
- 10 ice cubes
- 1 cup of frozen pineapple chunks
- ½ cup of water
- 1 tbsp lemon juice
- 1 banana
- 1 large green apple
- 1 cup of baby spinach or kale, loosely packed (or other chopped greens)

Instructions

1. Take out the pit from the avocado and put half of the flesh into the blender. Cut the apple into pieces, but don't peel it. Cut up the banana and put it and the milk in the blender. Put in the water and the young kale leaves. Mix until it's smooth.
2. Put in the lemon juice, frozen pineapple or mango, and ice. Remix it until it's smooth. If it separates, shake it back together. You can eat it right away or store it in a sealed jar for one to two days.

9. VEGAN MINT CHIP SMOOTHIE.

Total Time: 5 Minutes | Serving: 2

Ingredients

- 2 tsp raw coconut oil
- ½ tsp pure vanilla extract
- 1 tsp spirulina powder
- 2 pinches sea salt
- 2 drops of food-grade peppermint essential oil
- 2 cups of frozen banana chunks
- 1 tbsp shredded unsweetened coconut

- 1 ½ cups of milk of choice or 1 ½ cups of water + 2 tbsp hemp seeds
- 4 ice cubes
- dark chocolate shavings for garnish (optional)
- 2-3 tbsp raw cacao nibs plus extra for garnish
- 6 large fresh mint leaves plus extra for garnish

Instructions

1. Blend everything in the magic bullet blender, except for the cacao nibs, until it is completely smooth. Put the blender down and add the cacao nibs. It's up to you if you want the nibs to be chunky or smooth. You can add more cacao nibs, mint leaves, or dark chocolate shavings on top after you pour and serve.

10. CUCUMBER SMOOTHIE

Total Time: 5 Minutes | Serving: 2

Ingredients

- ½ cup of Greek yogurt (or coconut milk)
- 1 handful of spinach leaves
- 1 cup of peeled and chopped cucumber

- 1 ripe banana, broken into pieces
- 1 cup of frozen pineapple
- 10 ice cubes
- 1 tbsp lime juice or lemon juice (optional)

Instructions

2. Take the cucumber and cut it up. Put all ingredients into the Magic Bullet blender in the order given. Mix until it's smooth.
3. If it separates, shake it back together. You can eat it right away or store it in a sealed jar for one day.

11. GREEN SMOOTHIE RECIPE

Total Time: 5 Minutes | Serving: 1

Ingredients

- 1 cup of frozen fruit of choice
- 2 cups of greens
- 1–2 cups of liquid
- Nutritional add-ins: chia seeds, hemp seeds, protein powder, etc
- 1 frozen banana

Instructions

1. Using the magic bullet blender, put the liquid and greens in it and blend on high until there are no more green chunks.
2. Add the rest of the ingredients and blend until smooth and creamy, adding more liquid if needed.

12. PB BANANA AND CACAO GREEN SMOOTHIE

Total Time: 5 Minutes | Serving: 1

Ingredients

- 3/4 cup of unsweetened vanilla almond milk,
- 1/2 frozen ripe banana
- 1 cup of ice
- 2 tsp peanut butter
- 1 loose cup of baby spinach
- 1/3 ounce heaping tbsp cacao nibs
- optional a few drops of liquid stevia

Instructions

1. In a magic bullet blender, combine all ingredients and blend until smooth.

13. CITRUS GREEN SMOOTHIE

Total Time: 5 Minutes | Serving: 1

Ingredients

- 1/2 inch piece of fresh ginger root peeled
- 1 ounce organic baby spinach
- 3 ounces frozen mango chunks
- pinch finely ground sea salt
- 1 cup of plain unsweetened almond milk
- 1 tsp ground flax seeds
- 1 medium navel orange peeled
- 1 ounce walnuts
- 1 Medjool date pitted (optional for extra sweetness)

Instructions

1. Put all ingredients in your Magic Bullet blender jar in the order given. While mixing, keep going until the mixture is smooth and creamy. Serve right away and enjoy!

14. SPINACH, PEANUT BUTTER & BANANA SMOOTHIE

Total Time: 5 Minutes | Serving: 1

Ingredients

- 1 tbsp peanut butter
- 1 cup of spinach
- 1 cup of plain kefir
- 1 frozen banana
- 1 tbsp honey (Optional)

Instructions

1. Blend kefir, peanut butter, spinach, banana, and honey in a magic bullet blender. Mix until completely smooth.

15. KALE SMOOTHIE

Total Time: 5 Minutes | Serving: 2

Ingredients

- 1 tbsp fresh squeezed lemon juice
- 1 large green apple
- 1 banana
- ½ cup of water
- 2 cups of frozen pineapple or mango
- 2 cups of baby kale leaves, loosely packed (or Tuscan or curly kale, roughly chopped)
- 10 ice cubes

Instructions

1. Cut the apple into pieces, but don't peel it. Cut the bananas up and put them in the magic bullet blender. Put in the water and the young kale leaves. Mix until it's smooth.
2. Put in the lemon juice, frozen pineapple or mango, and ice. Remix it until it's smooth.

FRUIT SMOOTHIE

16. BANANA BLUEBERRY ORANGE SMOOTHIE

Total Time: 10 Minutes | Serving: 4

Ingredients

- 4 Tbsp medium orange, peeled
- 4 Tbsp small frozen bananas, peeled
- 1½ cups of frozen blueberries
- 3 cups of water

Instructions

1. Put the ingredients in the Magic Bullet container in the order given, and then screw the lid on tight.
2. Set the Magic Bullet blender to its slowest speed initially, then quickly raise it to its fastest setting.
3. Using the tamper to push the ingredients toward the blades, blend for 45 seconds or until your desired consistency is reached.

17. CRANBERRY AND ORANGE SMOOTHIE

Prep Time: 5 Minutes | Cook Time: 15 Minutes

Total Time: 20 Minutes | Serving: 2

Ingredients

- 1 cup of almond milk or whatever kind of milk you like
- ½ cup of whole milk Greek yogurt
- ⅔ cup of fresh or frozen cranberries
- 2 oranges peeled, seeded (I left in the seeds)
- 2 tbsp maple syrup

Instructions

1. Blend everything using your magic bullet blender until you get the desired texture.

18. APPLE SMOOTHIE

Total Time: 5 Minutes | Serving: 2

Ingredients

- 2 cups of fresh apple chunks
- 1 ripe banana, frozen (or at room temperature)
- ½ cup of Greek yogurt
- ¼ cup of milk (or almond milk or oat milk)
- 8 ice cubes
- ½ tsp vanilla extract
- ¼ tsp cinnamon
- Optional: ½ tbsp maple syrup or honey

Instructions

1. Cut up the apple. Break up the banana and put all ingredients into a Magic Bullet blender. Turn off the blender and scrape the sides as needed to make it creamy and frothy. If you want, you can add an apple slice as a garnish. You can serve it right away or put it in a jar with a lid and put it in the fridge for one day.

19. RASPBERRY SMOOTHIE

Total Time: 5 Minutes | Serving: 2

Ingredients

- 2 cups of frozen raspberries
- ½ cup of milk (or almond milk or oat milk)
- ½ cup of water
- ½ cup of ice
- For the garnish: Frozen raspberry, mint leaf
- 1 tbsp maple syrup or honey
- 1 banana (room temperature)
- ¼ cup of Greek yogurt

Instructions

1. Break up the banana and put all ingredients into a Magic Bullet blender. Add milk and blend until smooth, stopping to scrape down the sides as needed. You can add a frozen raspberry and mint leaf as a garnish. You can serve it right away or put it in a jar with a lid and put it in the fridge for one day.

20. BLACKBERRY KOMBUCHA SMOOTHIE

Total Time: 5 Minutes | Serving: 1

Ingredients

- 3 tbsp of agave or maple syrup
- 1/2 frozen banana, you can use a whole banana to make the smoothie a bit larger/ more filling
- 1 1/4 cups of kombucha,
- 1 cup of frozen blackberries or blueberries
- 1 cup of mango chunks, fresh or frozen
- 2 tbsp of lemon juice

Instructions

1. Put everything into a magic bullet blender and blend until it's smooth and creamy!
2. Serve right away and enjoy!

21. MANGO PINEAPPLE SMOOTHIE

Total Time: 5 Minutes | Serving: 2

Ingredients

- 1 drizzle maple syrup or honey, if desired
- 1/3 to 1/2 cup of milk
- 1 banana (room temperature, broken into chunks)
- 1 cup of frozen diced mango
- ½ cup of Greek yogurt
- ½ cup of ice cubes
- 1 ½ cups of fresh pineapple

Instructions

1. Break up the banana and put all ingredients in the magic bullet blender in the order given. Stop the blender and scrape down the sides as needed to make it creamy and foamy. If you need to, add a little more liquid.
2. If you think it needs it, add a drizzle of maple syrup based on how ripe your pineapple is. Most likely, you won't need it. You can serve it right away or put it in a jar with a lid and put it in the fridge for one day.

22. KIWI SMOOTHIE

Total Time: 5 Minutes | Serving: 1

Ingredients

- 2 kiwi
- 1 banana (room temperature)
- 2 handfuls of baby spinach or kale
- ¼ cup of water, plus more as needed
- ½ cup of Greek yogurt (or coconut milk for vegan, and omit the water)
- 1 ½ cups of frozen pineapple chunks

Instructions

1. Peel the kiwi and cut it up. Put everything into the Magic Bullet blender. Start by adding the liquids and then the solids. Break up the banana into pieces. If you need to, add more water and blend until smooth. You can eat it right away or put it in the fridge for up to one day in a covered jar.

23. HONEYDEW SMOOTHIE

Total Time: 10 Minutes | Serving: 2

Ingredients

- 1 pinch kosher salt
- 1/2 large honeydew melon (5 cups of diced)
- ¼ cup of Greek yogurt (or coconut milk o
- r vegan yogurt)
- 1 tsp honey (or maple syrup)
- ¼ cup of frozen pineapple (4 chunks)
- ¼ tsp vanilla extract
- Garnish: mint leaves (or add them to the smoothie, too!)

Instructions

1. Cut up the honeydew melon. Put it in a Magic Bullet blender and blend it for a few seconds to mix it all.
2. Blend the rest of the ingredients in until you get a pale green smoothie.

24. STRAWBERRY PINEAPPLE SMOOTHIE WITH BANANA

Total Time: 5 Minutes | Serving: 2

Ingredients

- 1 cup of frozen strawberries
- ½ cup of 100% unsweetened pineapple juice or orange juice
- 1 cup of frozen pineapple chunks
- 1/4 to 1/2 cup of milk
- ½ cup of ice
- ¼ cup of Greek yogurt
- 1 tbsp fresh lemon juice
- 1 banana (room temperature)

Instructions

1. Put everything into a Magic Bullet blender and break up the banana. Stop and scrape down the sides of the blender as needed, and add more milk if necessary to make it creamy and foamy. Add ½ to 1 tbsp of honey, maple, or agave syrup to make the smoothie sweeter. If you use pineapple or orange juice, you probably won't need it. You can eat it right away or put it in a jar with a lid and put it in the fridge for one day.

25. PEANUT BUTTER & JELLY SMOOTHIE

Total Time: 5 Minutes | Serving: 1

Ingredients

- 1 cup of frozen banana slices
- 1 cup of baby spinach
- ½ cup of low-fat milk
- ⅓ cup of nonfat plain Greek yogurt
- ½ cup of frozen strawberries
- 1 tbsp natural peanut butter
- 1-2 tsp pure maple syrup or honey (optional)

Instructions

1. In a Magic Bullet blender, combine milk and yogurt. Add spinach, banana, strawberries, peanut butter, and sweetener. Blend until consistency is smooth.

26. ACAI SMOOTHIE

Total Time: 5 Minutes | Serving: 1

Ingredients

- 4 tbsp of acai powder
- 2 frozen bananas (you could get away with only one)
- 1/2 cup of frozen strawberries
- 1/2 cup of frozen raspberries
- 1 tbsp of hemp seeds
- 1 cup of liquid, plus more as needed

Instructions

1. Using a magic bullet blender, blend all of the ingredients.
2. Enjoy!

27. PINEAPPLE GINGER SMOOTHIE

Total Time: 5 Minutes | Serving: 3

Ingredients

- 2 cups of spinach (or kale)
- 1/2 cup of frozen banana slices or mango
- 1 tsp fresh ginger or frozen ginger (peel removed)
- 1/2 cup of water (or more, if needed)
- 2 cups of frozen pineapple
- 2 tbsp chia seeds or collagen
- 1 cup of orange juice, or more if needed

Instructions

1. Add spinach, ginger, pineapple, banana or mango, chia seeds, or collagen, and blend them in the magic bullet blender.
2. Put water and orange juice in it.
3. Add more orange juice or water as needed while the mixture is covered and blended to make it smoother.

28. MANGO VANILLA SMOOTHIE

Total Time: 5 Minutes | Serving: 1

Ingredients

- 1 cup of frozen mango chunks
- 1/4 cup of vanilla soymilk
- 1/4 cup of 2 ounces plain Greek yogurt
- 1/2 tsp vanilla extract

Instructions

1. Mix all the ingredients in a magic bullet blender for about one minute or until smooth. Fill a tall glass or jar with the mixture. Hold it and enjoy it.

29. MANGO, COCONUT, AND DRAGON FRUIT SMOOTHIE

Prep Time: 20 Minutes | Cook Time: 15 Minutes

Total Time: 35 Minutes | Serving: 2

Ingredients

- 1 cup of coconut water, divided
- 2 cups of mango chunks, frozen
- 1 1/2 bananas, sliced and frozen, divided
- 1 Pitaya Plus pack
- 1 cup of coconut cream

Instructions

1. Put the mango, half a frozen banana, and 1/2 cup of coconut water in a powerful magic bullet blender. Mix until it's smooth, then split it between two glasses.
2. Clean your blender quickly. Mix the coconut cream, 1/4 cup of coconut water, and half a frozen banana in a blender. Mix until smooth, then pour on top of the mango layer in the glasses.
3. Clean your blender quickly. Mix the pitaya, 1/4 cup of coconut water, and half of a frozen banana in a blender. Blend until smooth, then pour on top of the coconut layer in the glasses.
4. Serve right away

30. WATERMELON SMOOTHIE

Total Time: 5 Minutes | Serving: 2

Ingredients

- 3 cups of cubed watermelon
- 10 ounces (2 heaping cups) frozen strawberries
- 1 banana, either frozen in slices or at room temp

Instructions

1. Cut up the watermelon. Put everything in a magic bullet blender until it's creamy and smooth. Serve right away.

31. PEANUT BUTTER BANANA SMOOTHIE

Total Time: 5 Minutes | Serving: 2

Ingredients

- ¼ cup of Old Fashioned oats
- 1 cup of ice
- 3/4 to 1 cup of milk of choice
- 3 tbsp peanut butter
- 1 tbsp pure maple syrup
- 2 medium ripe frozen bananas
- ½ tsp vanilla extract
- Protein adder: 1 scoop vanilla protein powder, optional

Instructions

1. Peel and cut the bananas. Then, freeze them for at least one and a half hours until solid.
2. Blend everything using a magic bullet blender by adding small amounts of milk until it all comes together. You can taste it and add maple syrup or honey.

32. BLACKBERRY SMOOTHIE

Total Time: 5 Minutes | Serving: 1

Ingredients

- ½ cup of plain whole-milk Greek yogurt
- 1 tsp finely chopped fresh ginger
- 1 tbsp honey
- 1 ½ tsp fresh lemon juice
- 1 cup of fresh blackberries (6 ounces)
- ½ medium banana

Instructions

1. Blend the ginger, blackberries, banana, yogurt, honey, lemon juice, and honey in a magic bullet blender. Put the lid on and process for about two minutes or until the mixture is completely smooth. Serve right away.

33. TIE-DYE FRUIT SMOOTHIE

Total Time: 10 Minutes | Serving: 2

Ingredients

Banana Smoothie Base:

- 1 1/2 Large Bananas
- 1 1/2 cups of Unsweetened Coconut Water

Raspberry Strawberry Smoothie:

- 1/4 up Frozen Raspberries
- 1/3 cup of Frozen Strawberries
- 1/4 of your Banana Smoothie Base

Carrot Ginger Smoothie:

- 1/2 a Carrot diced
- 1/4 inch piece of ginger peeled
- 1/4 of your Banana Smoothie Base

Mango Smoothie:

- 1/2 cup of Frozen Mango
- 1/4 of your Banana Smoothie Base

Blueberry Smoothie:

- 1/3 cup of Frozen Blueberries
- 1/4 of your Banana Smoothie Base

Instructions

1. Make the base for your banana smoothie: Bananas and coconut water should be blended in a Magic Bullet on High for a few seconds or until the mixture is smooth. Set aside after pouring into a measuring cup.
2. Mix Smoothies for Each Person: Include the ingredients for each smoothie and a quarter of the banana smoothie base in your Magic Bullet Jug. To make it even, blend it on high until it's smooth, then pour it into two glasses.
3. After each flavor, rinse the magic bullet jug and repeat it. Pour each layer on top of the last one to make a tie-dye effect.

34. PEACH SMOOTHIE

Total Time: 5 Minutes | Serving: 2

Ingredients

- 6 ice cubes
- ¼ cup of Greek yogurt
- 2 cups of frozen peaches
- 1 banana (room temperature)
- 1 cup of milk (or almond milk or oat milk)
- ½ tsp vanilla extract
- ¼ tsp cinnamon
- ½ tbsp maple syrup, honey, or agave syrup

Instructions

1. Put everything into a Magic Bullet blender and break up the banana. Turn off the blender and scrape the sides as needed to make it creamy and frothy. Add a frozen peach as a garnish if you want to. You can eat it right away or put it in a jar with a lid and put it in the fridge for one day.

35. BANANA AND DATE SMOOTHIE

Total Time: 5 Minutes | Serving: 15

Ingredients

- 250 ml milk, any soy for vegan option
- 1 cup of ice
- 1 banana peeled
- 20 g dates, dried, pitted
- 20 g almonds, raw

Instructions

1. Put 1 tbsp of hot water and dates in a small bowl. For five minutes, let the dates get soft.
2. Blend dates, milk, almonds, banana, and ice in a magic bullet blender. Mix until it's smooth.
3. Put it in a glass and enjoy!

36. APPLE SMOOTHIE WITH RASPBERRIES

Total Time: 5 Minutes | Serving: 2

Ingredients

- ½ cup of ice cubes
- 2 cups of apple, sliced, 1 large apple
- ½ cup of coconut water
- 2 medium bananas
- 2 cups of raspberries, frozen

Instructions

1. Put everything into a magic bullet blender.
2. Mix it for about 90 seconds or until it's smooth.
3. Add more coconut water or ice cubes if you want a thicker consistency.

37. CANTALOUPE SMOOTHIE

Total Time: 5 Minutes | Serving: 2

Ingredients

- 3 cups of cubed cantaloupe
- 1 cup of frozen pineapple
- ½ cup of Greek yogurt
- ½ cup of ice
- ½ cup of orange juice

Instructions

1. Using a magic bullet blender, blend the cantaloupe for a few seconds. After that, add all the other ingredients and blend until smooth. If necessary, add more orange juice while blending. Sample it, and if you'd like it sweeter, add some honey or pure maple syrup. Instantly serve. Refrigerate for up to one day; it will separate, so give it a good shake before serving.

38. BLUEBERRY CITRUS SMOOTHIE WITH SPINACH

Total Time: 5 Minutes | Serving: 2

Ingredients

- 1 small/medium orange
- 1 ½ cups of unsweetened almond milk
- ½ small grapefruit, about ½ cup
- 2 tbs plant-based vanilla protein powder
- 2 cups of frozen spinach
- 1 cup of blueberries frozen
- 1 banana frozen

Instructions

1. Put the ingredients into your Magic Bullet Blender in the order given.
2. Begin blending at a low speed and slowly raise it to a high speed.
3. Blend on high for 50 to 70 seconds or until all the ingredients are mixed in and the mixture is smooth.
4. Put it in cups of and serve right away!

39. FRUIT SMOOTHIE

Total Time: 5 Minutes | Serving: 2

Ingredients

- 1 cup of frozen pineapple or mango
- 1 tbsp maple syrup, honey, or agave syrup
- 10 ice cubes
- 1 banana
- 1 tbsp freshly squeezed lemon or lime juice
- 1 large green apple
- 2 cups of mixed berries
- 1 cup of water

Instructions

1. Cut the apple into chunks, but don't remove the core. Leave the skin on. Add it to the Magic Bullet blender first, then the banana that has been cut up.
2. Add the rest of the ingredients. Stop the blender and scrape it down as needed to make it smooth.

40. ORANGE BANANA SMOOTHIE

Total Time: 3 Minutes | Serving: 3

Ingredients

- 1-1/2 tsp maca root powder
- 1 tsp pure vanilla extract
- ¼ cup of unsweetened, shredded coconut
- ½ tsp turmeric
- 2 frozen bananas, cut in half
- 1-1/2 cups of coconut water
- 3 pitted dates
- ¼ cup of raw cashews
- 1 whole orange, with the peel, quartered
- 1 Tbs bee pollen granules

Instructions

1. Mix everything in a high-speed Magic Bullet blender.
2. Blend it until it's very smooth.
3. Put extra coconut flakes or orange slices on top if it makes you happy.
4. Enjoy!

41. ORANGE SMOOTHIE

Total Time: 5 Minutes | Serving: 1

Ingredients

- 2 large peeled oranges (or 3 medium)
- 1 banana (room temperature)
- ¼ cup of Greek yogurt
- 2 to 2 1/2 cups of ice
- ½ tsp vanilla extract
- ½ tbsp orange zest
- 1 tbsp maple syrup or honey (optional)

Instructions

1. About ½ orange zest. Put the orange peels, spice, banana, Greek yogurt, vanilla, maple syrup, or honey, and ice in a magic bullet blender. Mix until it's smooth.
2. You can eat it right away or keep it in the fridge for up to one day.

42. STRAWBERRY SMOOTHIE

Total Time: 5 Minutes | Serving: 2

Ingredients

- 1 cup of milk (or almond milk or oat milk)
- 1 ½ tbsp maple syrup, honey, or agave syrup
- ¼ cup of Greek yogurt
- 2 cups of frozen strawberries
- ½ cup of ice
- 1 banana (room temperature)
- Optional add-ins: 1 tbsp almond butter, ¼ tsp vanilla, fresh mint leaves or basil leaves

Instructions

1. Break up the banana and put all ingredients into a Magic Bullet blender. Turn off the blender and scrape the sides as needed to make it creamy and frothy. You can decorate it with a frozen strawberry and a mint sprig if you want to. You can serve it right away or put it in a jar with a lid and put it in the fridge for two days.

43. EVERYTHING SMOOTHIE

Total Time: 16 Minutes | Serving: 3

Ingredients

- 1 slice pineapple, peeled, halved
- 1 cup of ice cubes
- ½ cup of soy milk
- 1 cup of frozen strawberries
- 1 medium peach, halved, pitted
- ½ medium frozen banana
- ½ cup of fresh spinach
- 1 medium orange, peeled, halved
- ½ cup of red grapes
- ½ cup of broccoli florets
- 1 small carrot

Instructions

1. Put the ingredients in the Magic Bullet blender in order, then close the lid.
2. Set the Magic Bullet blender to its slowest speed at first and quickly raise it to its fastest setting. Press the ingredients toward the blades with the tamper for 50 seconds to blend them.

44. 4-INGREDIENT GRAPEFRUIT SMOOTHIE

Total Time: 60 seconds. | Serving: 2

Ingredients

- 1 whole peeled grapefruit
- 2 cups of frozen strawberries
- 1 whole cored apple
- 1 thumbnail-sized piece of ginger
- 4 ounces water (optional)

Instructions

1. Peel the grapefruit.
2. Apple core.
3. Put the soft fruit into the magic bullet blender.
4. Mix for one minute. Enjoy!

45. GREEN TEA MATCHA SMOOTHIE

Total Time: 5 Minutes | Serving: 2

Ingredients

- 1 cup of unsweetened almond milk
- 1 cup of baby spinach
- 1 cup of baby kale
- 1 tbsp matcha green tea powder
- 2 cups of ice cubes
- ½ cup of nonfat plain Greek yogurt or dairy-free
- ¼ cup of sliced almonds
- 1 banana, sliced
- 2 tsp natural sweetener

Instructions

1. Put everything into a magic bullet blender.
2. Mix it for about 60 to 90 seconds or until it's smooth. It's up to you whether you want to make the smoothie thicker by adding more ice or dairy milk.

46. GREEN TEA AND OAT SMOOTHIE

Total Time: 5 Minutes | Serving: 2

Ingredients

- 1 ripe banana, peeled
- 1/3 cucumber
- 1 large lettuce leaf
- 1 orange, peeled
- handful of Tuscan kale leaves
- 1/2 tsp matcha (green tea powder)
- 1/2 kiwifruit, peeled
- 1 cup of Greek yoghurt
- 1/2 cup of chilled water
- 1 tbsp instant oats
- handful of grapes

Instructions

1. Put everything in the Magic Bullet blender jug and blend until it's smooth and creamy.

47. BLUEBERRY BANANA SMOOTHIE

Total Time: 5 Minutes | Serving: 2

Ingredients

- 8 ice cubes
- ½ cup of water
- 1 tbsp fresh lemon juice
- 2 bananas (room temperature)
- 2 cups of frozen blueberries

Instructions

1. Put everything in a magic bullet blender and blend until smooth. If necessary, stop the side of the blender and scrape. If you need to, add more water to help it mix. Keep for up to one day in a jar that is tightly closed.

48. MANGO BANANA SMOOTHIE

Total Time: 5 Minutes | Serving: 2

Ingredients

- ½ cup of Greek yogurt
- 2 bananas (room temperature, broken into chunks)
- 1 ½ cups of frozen mango
- ½ cup of ice cubes
- 1/3 to 1/2 cup of milk

Instructions

1. Using a magic bullet blender, put all ingredients in the order given. As you add the bananas, break them up into pieces. Turn off the blender and scrape the sides as needed to make it creamy and frothy. Add a piece of mango or banana as a garnish if you want. You can serve it right away or put it in a jar with a lid and put it in the fridge for one day.

49. LEMON SMOOTHIE

Total Time: 5 Minutes | Serving: 2

Ingredients

- 1 banana (room temperature, broken into chunks)
- 2 cups of frozen pineapple
- 6 ice cubes
- 1 tsp maple syrup
- Zest of 1 lemon, plus 2 tbsp lemon juice
- 1 cup of milk of choice (or ½ cup of Greek yogurt and ½ cup of milk)
- 1/8 to 1/4 tsp turmeric (optional, for color)

Instructions

1. Put all ingredients into a Magic Bullet blender in the order given. Turn off the blender and scrape the sides as needed to make it creamy and frothy. If you need to, add a little more liquid.
2. If you think it needs it, add another drizzle of maple syrup based on how ripe your pineapple is. Most likely, you won't need it. You can serve it right away or put it in a jar with a lid and put it in the fridge for one day.

50. PINEAPPLE SMOOTHIE

Total Time: 5 Minutes | Serving: 2

Ingredients

- 5 ice cubes
- 3 cups of frozen pineapple
- 1/2 banana
- 1 ½ tbsp fresh squeezed lime juice (or lemon juice)
- ¾ cup of water
- ½ cup of milk (or almond milk or oat milk)

Instructions

1. Put everything except 1 cup of frozen pineapple in a magic bullet blender. Stop the blender and stir it occasionally until the mixture is smooth.
2. Blend it again after adding the last cup of frozen pineapple. Eat it immediately, or put it in a jar and seal it for one day.

51. STRAWBERRY-CHOCOLATE SMOOTHIE

Total Time: 5 Minutes | Serving: 1

Ingredients

- 1 cup of chilled unsweetened chocolate almond milk, plus more if needed
- 1 tbsp unsweetened cocoa powder
- 1 ½ cups of frozen strawberries
- 1 tbsp almond butter
- 1 tbsp honey

Instructions

1. Add honey, cocoa, almond milk, almond butter, and strawberries in a Magic Bullet blender. Put more almond milk if needed to get the consistency you want after processing until smooth. Serve right away.

52. GRAPE SMOOTHIE

Total Time: 5 Minutes | Serving: 2

Ingredients

- ½ cup of Greek yogurt (or ¼ cup of non-dairy milk for vegan)
- 1 banana (room temperature)
- 2 cups of seedless red grapes, frozen at least 2 hours or overnight
- ½ cup of milk (or almond milk or oat milk)

Instructions

1. Remember to freeze the grapes before you start the recipe!
2. Start with the milk and yogurt. Put everything into the Magic Bullet blender while breaking up the banana. If you need to, add a little more liquid to get the consistency you want. Blend until smooth.

53. PINK POWER SMOOTHIE

Total Time: 5 Minutes | Serving: 2

Ingredients

- 1 ½ cups of pink grapefruit flesh, rind removed
- 1 ½ cups of watermelon cubes, chilled or frozen
- 1 banana, frozen
- 2 tsp sprouted raw pumpkin seeds, salted
- ¼ cup of coconut water (or try guava juice for more pink power!)
- 1 tsp liquid sweetener (optional)
- spicy version: add cayenne or some raw grated ginger

Instructions

1. Put watermelon, grapefruit, coconut water, and a sweetener into the Magic Bullet blender. Blend until smooth. To puree smoothly, you will need to use a high speed. Blend the frozen banana in until it is smooth and frosty. To serve, pour it over and sprinkle pumpkin seeds on top.

54. GOLD MEDAL SMOOTHIE

Total Time: 10 Minutes | Serving: 2

Ingredients

- 2 cups of ice cubes
- 1/4 medium orange, peeled
- 1/2 small carrots
- 1 medium banana, peeled
- 1/2 cup of cantaloupe chunks
- 1/2 cup of water
- ¼ lemon, peeled
- ⅛ tsp ground nutmeg
- 1 slice pineapple, peeled, halved
- 2 dates (or 1 tbsp honey, optional), pitted

Instructions

1. Put the ingredients in the Magic Bullet container in the order given, and then close the lid.
2. Set the Magic Bullet blender to its slowest speed first, then raise it to its fastest speed.
3. Press the ingredients toward the blades with the tamper for 1 minute or until the desired consistency is reached. Serve right away.

55. DRAGON FRUIT SMOOTHIE

Total Time: 5 Minutes | Serving: 5

Ingredients

- 1 cup of frozen pineapple chunks
- 1 large banana (room temperature)
- ½ cup of cold water
- 7 ounces frozen dragonfruit puree (two 3.5-ounce packets)
- ½ cup of frozen diced or fresh mango
- 1 tbsp lime juice (optional)

Instructions

1. Let the dragonfruit puree thaw in warm water until it can be broken up into smaller pieces. Put the pieces out of the packaging in the magic bullet blender. Put in the water first, then the chunked pineapple, mango, and banana.
2. Turn off and scrape the sides of the bowl as needed to make the mixture smooth. If you need to, add a little more cold water to turn the frozen mango into a puree.
3. If you want to, taste it and then add the lime juice. Immediately serve or store in a covered jar for up to 1 day

56. BERRY-KEFIR SMOOTHIE

Total Time: 5 Minutes | Serving: 1

Ingredients

- 1 cup of plain kefir
- 2 tsp almond butter
- ½ tsp vanilla extract
- 1 ½ cups of frozen mixed berries
- ½ medium banana

Instructions

1. Mix the berries, kefir, banana, almond butter, and vanilla in a Magic Bullet blender. Blend until it's smooth.

57. CHERRY SMOOTHIE

Total Time: 5 Minutes | Serving: 1

Ingredients

- 1/2 cup of yogurt of choice
- 1 cup of liquid
- 1 cup of frozen cherries
- 2/3 cup of frozen cauliflower OR 1 medium banana, preferably frozen
- 1 heaping tbsp of almond butter or other nut butter (optional but recommended!)

Instructions

1. Put everything into your Magic Bullet blender and blend it until it's smooth. If you need to thin it out a bit, add more liquid. Put a few ice cubes in the smoothie to make it thicker if you use fresh cherries.
2. Have fun!

58. PINEAPPLE CUCUMBER SMOOTHIE

Total Time: 5 Minutes | Serving: 1

Ingredients

- 1/2 large ripe, peeled, frozen banana
- 1/2 cup of sliced cucumber
- 1/2 cup of filtered water
- 1 large handful greens
- 1/4 cup of light coconut milk
- 1 medium lime, zested + juiced
- 1 heaping cup of cubed pineapple
- 2-4 ice cubes

Instructions

1. Put the ice cubes, lime zest, lime juice, frozen banana, cucumber, pineapple, light coconut milk, water, greens, and ice in a Magic Bullet blender. Mix on high speed until it's smooth and creamy. If you need to, stop and scrape down the sides.
2. Put in more ice to make the smoothie thicker. Add more liquid to your smoothie if you want it to be thinner. Put more lime juice or zest if you want it to be more acidic or bright. If you want it sweeter, add more banana or pineapple. Add more coconut milk if you want it creamier. If you want it to be green, add more greens.
3. Serve right away. Covered leftovers can stay in the fridge for up to 24 hours, but they taste best when fresh.

59. CHERRY, PISTACHIO, CARDAMOM KOMBUCHA SMOOTHIE

Total Time: 5 Minutes | Serving: 2.5

Ingredients

- 2 tbsp pistachios, shelled
- ½ tsp ground cardamom
- 1½ cup of kombucha
- 1 cup of frozen peach slices, (thawed)
- 1 cup of frozen cherries
- ½ tbsp banana, peeled, halved
- 1 tbsp honey, optional

Instructions

1. Put all the ingredients in the Magic Bullet container in the order given, then secure the lid.
2. Select Variable 1.
3. After turning on the Magic Bullet Blender, slowly raise the speed until it reaches Variable 10, then raise it again to High.
4. Blend for 1 minute and 20 seconds or until your desired consistency is reached.

60. BEET SMOOTHIE

Total Time: 5 Minutes | Serving: 2

Ingredients

- 1 small raw beet (about 2/3 cup of peeled and diced)
- ½ cup of water
- 10 ice cubes
- 1 large green apple
- 1 banana
- 1 cup of frozen pineapple chunks or mango

Instructions

1. Peel the raw beet and cut it into dice. Be careful with the beet juice because it stains!
2. Cut the apple into pieces, but don't peel it. Cut the banana into little pieces.
3. Put in the ice cubes, apple, banana, frozen pineapple, and beet. Using a magic bullet blender, blend until it's smooth. Immediately eat or store for 1 day in a sealed jar; if it separates, shake it to bring it back together.

61. CHAI-SPICED BUTTERNUT SQUASH SMOOTHIE

Total Time: 10 Minutes | Serving: 1

Ingredients

- 1 cup of unsweetened almond milk or coconut milk
- 1 cup of cooked/roasted and frozen butternut squash
- ⅛ tsp allspice
- ¼ cup of plain or vanilla Greek yogurt
- 1 tbsp almond, cashew or pecan butter
- 1 frozen ripe banana
- ⅛ tsp cardamom
- ½ tsp cinnamon
- ⅛ tsp ground ginger
- ½ tsp vanilla extract

Instructions

1. Blend all the ingredients in a large, high-powered Magic Bullet blender. Blend high for 1 to 2 minutes or until everything is well mixed. If you need to thin it out, add more milk and blend again.

62. CINNAMON SWEET POTATO PIE SMOOTHIE

Total Time: 5 Minutes | Serving: 1

Ingredients

- ½ cup of plain Greek yogurt
- 1 frozen banana
- 1 cup of frozen cubed sweet potato
- 1 tbsp almond butter or pecan butter
- Pinch of ground cloves
- 1 tsp vanilla extract
- Pinch of nutmeg
- ¾ cup of unsweetened almond milk, plus more as necessary
- ½ tsp ground cinnamon

Instructions

1. Combine all the ingredients in a large, high-powered magic bullet blender. Blend high for 1 to 2 minutes or until everything is well mixed. For a thinner smoothie, add more almond milk. If you want, you can drizzle it with almond butter and top it with your favorite granola.

63. PUMPKIN SMOOTHIE

Total Time: 5 Minutes | Serving: 2

Ingredients

- 1 cup of ice cubes
- 1 tsp vanilla extract
- 1 ½ cups of fresh apple chunks
- 1 ½ tbsp maple syrup
- ½ cup of Greek yogurt or plain yogurt
- 1 tsp Pumpkin Pie Spice
- ½ cup of pumpkin puree
- 1 medium ripe banana
- For the topping: pumpkin pie spice, maple pecan granola, etc.

Instructions

1. Put the ingredients into the Magic Bullet blender. As you add the banana, break it up into pieces.
2. Blend on high until smooth and thoroughly pureed. Stop and scrape the sides as needed. It depends on your blender and the yogurt's texture if you need to add milk or water to get it going. Eat it immediately or put it in the fridge for up to a day.

64. BEET & BERRY SMOOTHIE

Total Time: 5 Minutes | Serving: 2

Ingredients

- 2/3 cup of fresh apple juice
- 1 ⅓ cup of frozen strawberries
- 1/3 cup of peeled + chopped raw beet
- 1/4 ripe frozen banana (optional)
- Fresh mint or shredded coconut (optional)

Instructions

1. Put the beet, strawberries, banana (optional for sweetness), and apple juice in a Magic Bullet blender. Mix on high speed until it's smooth and creamy. If you need to, stop and scrape down the sides.
2. If you want it sweeter, add more bananas. If you want it thinner, add more apple juice. If you want a stronger fruit flavor, add more strawberries.
3. Put some in each of the 2 glasses and enjoy. You can add banana slices, fresh mint, or shredded coconut as a garnish if you want to. It's best when fresh, but you can cover leftovers and keep them in the fridge for up to 2 days. Set aside leftovers in ice cubes or popsicle molds for a pick-me-up in the afternoon.

65. CUCUMBER MELON SMOOTHIE

Total Time: 20 Minutes | Serving: 3

Ingredients

- 1 cup of green grapes
- ½ small cucumber
- 1 small lime, peeled
- 1½ cup of cantaloupe, peeled, seeded
- ¼ cup of soy milk , or alternative milk
- 1 cup of ice cubes
- 1 cup of honeydew melon, peeled, seeded

Instructions

1. Put the ingredients into the Magic Bullet container in the given order, then lock the lid on tight.
2. Put the Magic Bullet blender on its slowest speed first, then raise it to its fastest speed.
3. Push the ingredients toward the blades with the tamper and blend for 45 seconds or until your desired consistency is reached.

66. CARROT SMOOTHIE

Total Time: 5 Minutes | Serving: 2

Ingredients

- 1 large apple, chopped into cubes
- ½ cup of orange juice
- ½ cup of frozen pineapple or mango
- 10 ice cubes
- 1 banana (room temperature)
- 1 cup of thinly sliced carrot rounds
- Optional mix in: ½ tsp grated fresh ginger, ¼ tsp cinnamon

Instructions

1. Cut the carrots into rounds after peeling them. Cut up the apple, but don't take off the peel. Cut the banana into little pieces.
2. Put all of the ingredients into the magic bullet blender. Start by adding the liquids. Mix until it's smooth. Drink it immediately or put it in the fridge in a covered jar for up to 1 day.

67. CHERRY-SPINACH SMOOTHIE

Total Time: 5 Minutes | Serving: 1

Ingredients

- 1 tbsp salted almond butter
- 1 cup of plain low-fat kefir
- ¼ cup of mashed ripe avocado
- 1 cup of frozen cherries
- 1 (1/2 inch) piece peeled ginger
- ½ cup of baby spinach leaves
- 1 tsp chia seeds, plus more for garnish

Instructions

1. Using a Magic Bullet blender, blend the kefir. Add the chia seeds, almond butter, spinach, avocado, cherries, and ginger. Blend until your mixture is smooth. Pour into a glass and top with more chia seeds if you want.

68. BLUEBERRY CAULIFLOWER SMOOTHIE

Total Time: 3 Minutes | Serving: 4

Ingredients

- 1 ripe banana
- 1 cup of frozen cauliflower rice
- 1 cup of water
- ¼ cup of almond butter or peanut butter, can sub sunflower butter to make nut-free
- 2 cups of oat milk, or milk of choice
- 2 cups of frozen blueberries
- 2 tbsp chia seeds, optional

Instructions

1. Mix frozen cauliflower, water, and milk with a Magic Bullet blender. Blend the cauliflower until it is completely pureed.
2. Put the rest of the ingredients into a blender. Gradually speed up the blender and blend until the mixture is smooth. If you need to, add a little more water until you get the consistency you want.
3. Pour into glasses and drink right away.

DETOX SMOOTHIE

69. PINEAPPLE DETOX SMOOTHIE

Total Time: 10 Minutes | Serving: 4

Ingredients

- 1 cup of frozen banana chunks
- 2 cups of ice
- 1 lemon, peel cut off
- 1 cucumber, peeled
- 10 ounce bag of frozen peach slices
- 1 cup of fresh pineapple chunks
- 1-2" piece of fresh ginger, peeled
- 2 stalks of celery (optional)

Instructions

1. Put the lemon, cucumber, and pineapple at the bottom of the blender. Because these are liquids, the Magic Bullet blender will need them at the bottom to help blend.
2. Blend the peaches, ginger, banana, and celery until smooth.
3. Blend in ice until the desired texture is achieved.
4. Pour into glasses and serve right away.
5. Refrigerate leftovers in a mason jar. When you're ready to drink, mix them with ice.

70. CLEANSING APPLE AVOCADO SMOOTHIE

Total Time: 5 Minutes | Serving: 2

Ingredients

- 4 cups of loosely packed spinach
- 1 medium avocado peeled and pitted
- 1 cup of plain unsweetened almond milk
- Small handful of ice cubes
- 1/2 tsp ground ginger or 1/4-inch knob of fresh ginger
- 2 tsp honey or maple syrup plus additional to taste
- 1 medium banana cut into chunks and frozen
- 2 medium apples any kind you like, peel on, cored, and quartered
- Optional additions: chia seeds flaxseed, protein powder, almond butter or other nut butter of choice

Instructions

1. Put the almond milk, spinach, avocado, apples, banana, honey, ginger, and ice in a high-powered Magic Bullet blender in the order given.
2. Mix until it's smooth. Taste it and change the amount of sugar and spices as you like. Enjoy right away.

71. GREEN APPLE DETOX SMOOTHIE

Total Time: 5 Minutes | Serving: 2

Ingredients

- 1 medium banana
- 1 medium green apple
- 2 cups of frozen pineapple
- 1/2 medium lemon, juiced
- 2 cups of frozen kale
- 1-2 tbsp grated ginger (or 1/2 tsp ginger powder)
- 2-3 stalks celery
- 1 1/2 cups of coconut water

Instructions

1. Blend the kale, coconut water, and ginger.
2. Use a Magic Bullet blender to blend the rest of the ingredients until the mixture is smooth.
3. Serve and have fun!

72. ORANGE GINGER DETOX SMOOTHIE

Total Time: 5 Minutes | Serving: 2

Ingredients

- 2 tbsp Flax Seeds
- 1 large orange (seedless, peeled)
- ½ cup of water
- 1 cup of shredded carrots
- 3-inch piece ginger (thinly sliced)
- ⅔ cup of protein powder (any flavor)
- ¼ cup of lemon juice
- ice to taste

Instructions

1. Put everything in a high-speed Magic Bullet blender and blend it until it's smooth. Keep adding ice until you get the right consistency to make it thicker.

73. GREEN TEA WATERMELON DETOX SMOOTHIE

Prep Time: 5 Minutes | Cook Time: 2 Minutes

Total Time: 7 Minutes | Serving: 2

Ingredients

- 1 cup of water
- 2 tbsp honey
- 1 tsp lemon juice - 1 tsp
- 2 cups of chilled watermelon, roughly chopped
- 7-8 ice cubes
- 2 green tea bags

Instructions

1. Boil some water, then pour it over the tea bags. Let them sit for 4 minutes.
2. Squeeze the tea bags out and set them aside to cool for 4 hours or overnight.
3. Put everything in a Magic Bullet blender and blend it until it's smooth.
4. Place ice cubes in glasses and pour smoothie on top of them.
5. Serve right away.

74. DETOX SPINACH GREEN SMOOTHIE

Total Time: 10 Minutes | Serving: 2

Ingredients

- 2 bananas
- 1 apple
- 1 lemon
- 1 cup of water, or as needed
- 1 cup of baby spinach

Instructions

1. Use a magic bullet to blend bananas and an apple that has been peeled and cut into slices.
2. Clean the baby spinach and put it in the blender.
3. Add 1 lemon juice to the blender. You can use orange or lime juice if you'd rather not use lemon juice.
4. Add about a cup of water if you need to.
5. Mix until smooth, then serve.

75. TROPICAL PAPAYA DETOX SMOOTHIE

Total Time: 5 Minutes | Serving: 2

Ingredients

- 2 Medjool Dates, pits removed
- 1/2 Large Papaya, cut into cubes
- 2 tbsp Unsweetened Coconut Shavings plus more as desired
- z1.5 cups of Coconut Milk, plus more as needed
- 1 cup of Frozen Pineapple
- 1 1/2 cups of Frozen Mango
- 1/2 tsp Ground Turmeric, optional

Instructions

1. Put the ingredients into a powerful Magic Bullet blender until smooth.
2. Add more non-dairy milk if you want your smoothie to be thinner. Put more frozen fruit or ice to your smoothie and blend until it's your desired consistency.

76. GINGER PEACH DETOX SMOOTHIE

Total Time: 5 Minutes | Serving: 2

Ingredients

- 1-inch piece of fresh ginger, peeled
- ⅓ cup of frozen strawberries
- 2 cups of frozen peaches
- 1 cup of cold water
- 1 medium cucumber, peeled
- 1 lemon, peeled
- 1 orange, peeled
- 1 apple, cored
- 2 cups of ice

Instructions

1. Put everything except the ice in a high-speed Magic Bullet blender and blend until smooth.
2. Add the ice and blend it in again to mix.

77. BLUEBERRY DETOX SMOOTHIE

Total Time: 10 Minutes | Serving: 1

Ingredients

- 1/2 cup of orange juice
- 1/4 avocado
- 1 small handful fresh cilantro leaves
- 1 cup of frozen wild blueberries
- 1 frozen banana, cut into pieces for easy blending
- 1/4 cup of water

Instructions

1. Blend the blueberries, cilantro, banana, avocado, orange juice, and water using a Magic Bullet blender until the mixture is completely smooth. Serve right now.

78. SUPERFOOD GREEN DETOX SMOOTHIE

Total Time: 10 Minutes | Serving: 4

Ingredients

- 1 cup of Swiss chard chopped, about 5 leaves, without the stems
- 1 cup of pomegranate seeds seeded, or juice with a citrus juicer as some blender might not blend the seeds well
- ¼ avocado pit, and skin removed
- ½ cup of spinach
- 1 tbsp ginger fresh, peeled and grated
- 3 Medjool dates pitted
- 1 ¾ cups of coconut milk unsweetened lite

Optional:

- 2 tsp maca powder for improved mood
- 8 ice cubs

- 2 tbsp Organic Protein Plant-Based Powder
- 1 tbsp flax meal for extra antioxidants
- ½ banana for extra sweetness

Instructions

1. Cut the avocado in half and take out the pulp.To make the Meedjol dates, peel the ginger and take out the pits.Take the Swiss chard stems off and set them aside for another recipe.
2. Take the pomegranate seeds out of the fruit and remove the white flesh.
3. Put spinach, Swiss chard, avocado, and pomegranate seeds scooped into the Magic Bullet blender in that order.
4. Add the ice cubes and coconut milk. Mix the fresh ginger with the honey.
5. Add more water or coconut milk as needed to get the right consistency after blending until the mixture is completely smooth. Drink it immediately, or put it in a mason jar with a closed lid.

79. TRIPLE CHOCOLATE DETOX SMOOTHIE

Total Time: 10 Minutes | Serving: 2

Ingredients

- 1 cup of unsweetened vanilla almond milk
- 1 cup of kale
- ½ tbsp raw honey
- ¼ cup of finely chopped dark chocolate , bittersweet or semisweet

- ½ avocado sliced
- 1 tbsp coconut oil
- 1 frozen banana chopped
- ⅓ cup of Chocolate Protein Powder
- 1 tbsp unsweetened cocoa powder
- 1 cup of water

Instructions

1. Blend everything with a large, powerful Magic Bullet blender until smooth. If it's too thick, add more water or almond milk and blend again.

80. STRAWBERRY KIWI CITRUS BURST

Total Time: 10 Minutes | Serving: 5

Ingredients

- 1 kiwifruit, sliced
- 1 1/2 tsp honey
- 1 banana sliced
- 5 frozen whole strawberries
- 1 1/4 cup of apple juice

Instructions

1. Put the banana, kiwifruit, strawberries, apple juice, and honey in a Magic Bullet blender. Blend until smooth and thick. Serve by pouring into tall glasses.

81. BRAIN FOOD SMOOTHIE

Total Time: 15 Minutes | Serving: 6

Ingredients

- 1 cup of fresh baby spinach
- 2 medium ripe avocados, peeled and pitted
- 1-1/2 cups of fat-free vanilla Greek yogurt
- 2 cups of halved fresh strawberries
- 1/2 cup of 2% milk
- 1/4 cup of unflavored whey protein powder
- 1 cup of sliced ripe banana
- 1/2 cup of fresh or frozen blackberries, thawed
- 1 cup of fresh blueberries
- 1 cup of fresh raspberries or frozen unsweetened raspberries, thawed

Instructions

1. Mix everything in a Magic Bullet blender, then cover it and blend until smooth.

82. BERRY SMOOTHIE

Total Time: 5 Minutes | Serving: 2

Ingredients

- 1 cup of milk (or almond milk or oat milk)
- 1 banana (room temperature)
- 2 cups of frozen mixed berries
- ½ cup of ice
- 1 ½ tbsp maple syrup, honey, or agave syrup
- ½ cup of Greek yogurt
- Optional add-ins: 1 tbsp almond butter, ¼ tsp vanilla, fresh mint leaves or basil leaves

Instructions

1. Break up the banana and put all ingredients into a Magic Bullet blender. Turn off the blender and scrape down the sides. If you need to, add a little more milk to get it to blend again. You can decorate it with a frozen strawberry and a mint sprig if you want to. You can serve it immediately or put it in a jar with a lid in the fridge for 2 days.

83. KALE PINEAPPLE SMOOTHIE

Total Time: 5 Minutes | Serving: 2

Ingredients

- 1 cup of kale frozen or fresh
- 1 banana frozen or fresh
- 1 cup of water or nut milk
- 1 tsp chia seeds
- 1 cup of pineapple frozen or fresh
- 1 tsp spirulina powder, optional

Instructions

1. Put everything into your Magic Bullet blender and blend until it's smooth. Adding the liquid little by little will help you get the right consistency. Don't add it all at once.

84. CHOCOLATE PEANUT BUTTER BANANA OATMEAL SMOOTHIE

Total Time: 5 Minutes | Serving: 2

Ingredients

- ½ - 1 tbs unsweetened cocoa powder
- 1 ½ cups of unsweetened vanilla almond milk
- 2 cups of kale frozen
- 2 tbs old-fashioned oats
- 3 Dates pitted
- 1 TBS creamy peanut butter
- 1 banana frozen
- 2 cups of frozen spinach

Instructions

1. Put the ingredients in your magic bullet blender in the order it says on the container.
2. Select "smoothie" and let it blend.
3. If your Magic Bullet doesn't have a smoothie setting, blend on low and work your way up to high speed.
4. Blend for 50 to 60 seconds until the mixture is smooth and all ingredients are mixed.
5. Serve right away!

85. BERRY BREAKFAST SMOOTHIES

Total Time: 5 Minutes | Serving: 5

Ingredients

- 2 containers (6 ounces each) raspberry yogurt
- 8 ice cubes
- 1 cup of frozen unsweetened blueberries
- 1 cup of frozen unsweetened raspberries
- 2 cups of cranberry juice

Instructions

1. Put all of the ingredients into a Magic Bullet blender. Cover it and blend for 30 to 45 seconds or until smooth. Put into chilled glasses and serve right away.

86. MANGO GINGER SMOOTHIES

Total Time: 5 Minutes | Serving: 4

Ingredients

- 2 medium ripe bananas, peeled and halved
- 1 package (16 ounces) frozen mango chunks
- 1 to 2 tsp minced fresh ginger root
- 1 tbsp honey
- 1-1/2 cups of cold water
- 1 tbsp coconut oil, melted

Instructions

1. Put everything in a Magic Bullet blender and blend until it's smooth. Put into chilled glasses and serve right away.

87. BANANA-MANGO SMOOTHIE

Total Time: 5 Minutes | Serving: 2

Ingredients

- 1 tsp honey
- ¾ cup of sliced ripe banana (about 1 medium)
- ¼ tsp vanilla extract
- 1 cup of cubed peeled ripe mango
- ⅔ cup of fat-free milk
- 1 tbsp nonfat dry milk (optional)

Instructions

1. Put the mango cubes on a baking sheet in a single layer. Freeze for about an hour or until they are firm. Use a Magic Bullet blender to blend frozen mango, banana, milk, dry milk (if using), honey, and vanilla extract. Mix until smooth.

88. TROPICAL SMOOTHIE

Total Time: 5 Minutes | Serving: 2

Ingredients

- ½ cup of orange juice (or pineapple juice, for a sweeter smoothie)
- 6 ice cubes
- 1 ½ cups of frozen pineapple
- 1 cup of frozen mango
- 1 ripe banana
- 2/3 cup of canned coconut milk
- Coconut flakes, for garnish (or to blend)

Instructions

1. Break up the banana and put all ingredients into a Magic Bullet blender. Turn off the blender and scrape down the sides as needed. If you need to, add more coconut milk or juice. Blend until smooth and foamy.
2. Taste it and change the flavors as you like. For example, add some honey for more sweetness or coconut flakes for a stronger coconut flavor. You can serve it immediately or put it in a jar with a lid in the fridge for 2 days. If the smoothie separates, give it a good shake.

89. TRIPLE BERRY SMOOTHIE

Total Time: 10 Minutes | Serving: 2

Ingredients

- 1 cup of frozen strawberries
- 1 cup of frozen blueberries
- 1 cup of frozen raspberries
- 1 cup of water
- 1 cup of red grapes
- 1 cup of almond yogurt, or low-fat vanilla yogurt

Instructions

1. Put the ingredients in the Magic Bullet container in the order given, and then close the lid.
2. Set the Magic Bullet blender to its slowest speed first, then raise it to its fastest speed.
3. Push the ingredients toward the blades with the tamper, and blend for 1 minute or until the desired consistency is reached.

90. COCONUT & BERRY COLLAGEN SMOOTHIE

Total Time: 5 Minutes | Serving: 2

Ingredients

- 1 tsp. 100% vanilla extract
- 1/2 avocado
- 2 cups of coconut milk
- 3 tbs. frozen blueberries
- 1 tsp. cinnamon
- 1 cup of ice
- 1 tb Nutraviva Collagen powder

Instructions

1. Use the magic bullet blender to mix everything.
2. Mix until it's smooth!
3. Enjoy this good for you collagen smoothie.

91. CREAMY WATERMELON SMOOTHIE

Total Time: 10 Minutes | Serving: 4

Ingredients

- 4 cups of seeded cubed watermelon, partially frozen
- 1/2 cup of fat-free milk
- 1/2 cup of reduced-fat vanilla ice cream
- 6 fresh mint leaves
- 1 tbsp sugar

Instructions

1. Put all ingredients in a Magic Bullet blender and blend until smooth.

92. PLUM SMOOTHIE

Total Time: 10 Minutes | Serving: 2

Ingredients

- 5 large ice cubes (or until cold)
- 1/2 cup of milk of choice
- 1/2 tsp ground ginger
- 2 large plums, pit removed (ripe!)
- 1 large orange, peeled
- 1/4 tsp cinnamon
- 2 tbsp chia seeds
- 1 tsp vanilla extract
- 3/4 cup of plain Greek yogurt

Instructions

1. Add all ingredients to a high-speed Magic Bullet blender, starting with the milk.
2. Set the blender to high speed and blend until smooth and creamy. You can change the flavors or the amount of liquid until you get the desired taste and consistency. Have fun!

93. POMEGRANATE SMOOTHIE

Total Time: 5 Minutes | Serving: 2

Ingredients

- 1 cup of pomegranate juice
- 1 large banana
- 1 cup of pears, diced
- 1 cup of ice cubes
- 2 tsp minced ginger
- 2 cups of frozen strawberries
- ¼ cup of pomegranate arils

Instructions

1. Put everything into a Magic Bullet blender.
2. Mix it for about 90 seconds or until it's smooth.
3. If you need to, add more ice cubes or pomegranate juice to make the mixture thick and creamy.
4. Put some of the mixture into 2 glasses. If you want, you can add more pomegranate juice, arils, and diced pears on top.

94. PINK POWER PROTEIN SMOOTHIE

Prep Time: 2 Minutes | Cook Time: 2 Minutes

Total Time: 4 Minutes | Serving: 1

Ingredients

- 1 small raw beet, peeled and quartered
- 1 tsp raw honey
- 1 banana
- 1 tbsp flaxseed meal
- 1 cup of unsweetened almond milk
- 1 cup of frozen strawberries
- 1 scoop vanilla protein powder (optional)

Instructions

1. Put the frozen banana, flaxseed meal, raw honey, a small raw beet that has been peeled, and a frozen strawberry in a Magic Bullet blender.
2. Mix everything until it's very smooth.
3. You can also add protein powder.

95. OATMEAL SMOOTHIE

Total Time: 5 Minutes | Serving: 1

Ingredients

- ½ cup of rolled oats
- 1 frozen banana (sliced)
- ¾ cup of milk (any kind)
- ½ cup of plain nonfat Greek yogurt
- 1 Medjool date (pitted)
- ¼ tsp ground cinnamon

Instructions

1. Add a Medjool date, a frozen banana, rolled oats, ground cinnamon, and milk to the Magic Bullet blender. Close the lid.
2. In the order given, put the ingredients into the blender.
3. Mix until it's smooth.
4. Put the blender on low speed for 10 seconds, starting it up. For 1 minute, turn up the speed to high.
5. Pour the smoothie into a cup. Serve right away.

96. STRAWBERRY PROTEIN SMOOTHIE

Total Time: 5 Minutes | Serving: 1

Ingredients

- 1 cup of unsweetened almond milk
- 1 tbsp hemp seeds
- 1 ¼ cups of frozen strawberries
- 1 scoop vanilla protein powder

Instructions

1. Add frozen strawberries, vanilla protein powder, hemp seeds, and unsweetened almond milk to a Magic Bullet blender. Lock the lid.
2. For 10 seconds, start the blender at low speed. For 1 minute, turn up the high speed. Blend until it's smooth.
3. Pour the smoothie into a cup. Serve right away.

97. BANANA PROTEIN SMOOTHIE

Total Time: 5 Minutes | Serving: 1

Ingredients

- 1 scoop vanilla protein powder
- 1 cup of oat milk
- 1 tbsp chia seeds
- 1 ½ frozen bananas (sliced)

Instructions

1. Use a Magic Bullet blender to blend frozen bananas, vanilla protein powder, oat milk, and chia seeds. Lock the lid.
2. Start the blender on low for 10 seconds. Speed up to high for 1 minute. Mix it up until it's smooth.
3. Pour the smoothie into a cup. Serve right away.

98. CHOCOLATE NUT BANANA PROTEIN SMOOTHIE

Total Time: 5 Minutes | Serving: 1

Ingredients

- 2 tbsp peanut, almond or cashew butter
- 1 small frozen banana
- 1 tbsp cocoa powder
- 2 tbsp vanilla, chocolate or unflavored protein powder
- 1 cup of Silk Almond Milk
- 1 tbsp coconut sugar (optional)

Instructions

1. Put everything in a Magic Bullet blender and blend it until it's smooth. Pour it into a large glass. Add sliced or slivered almonds, cocoa powder, and a sprig of mint as a garnish if you like. Serve right away.

99. GREEN PROTEIN SMOOTHIE

Total Time: 5 Minutes | Serving: 2

Ingredients

- 1 ½ cups of unsweetened almond milk
- 1 medium banana frozen
- 2 cups of frozen spinach
- 1 cup of fruit of choice
- Optional add ins: protein powder bee pollen, collagen, etc.

Instructions

1. Put the ingredients into the Magic Bullet blender's container in the order given.
2. Start blending on low and then raise the speed to high.
3. Blend at high speed for 50 to 60 seconds, or until the mixture is smooth.
4. Pour into glasses and have fun!

100. VANILLA BEAN PROTEIN SMOOTHIE

Total Time: 5 Minutes | Serving: 1

Ingredients

- 2 tbsp powdered nut butter
- 1 cup of unsweetened almond or cashew milk
- 1 frozen banana
- 1 tsp vanilla extract
- 1 scoop vanilla protein powder
- optional: sprinkles or your favorite topping

Instructions

1. Using a Magic Bullet blender, mix all of the ingredients.
2. Add 2 ice cubes to the blender or serve over ice if you want to.
3. You can add sprinkles or your favorite fun topping if you want to.

IMMUNE SYSTEM SMOOTHIES

101. EMERALD SMOOTHIE

Total Time: 11 Minutes | Serving: 3

Ingredients

- ½ cup of low-fat vanilla yogurt
- 2 cups of ice cubes
- 3 slices pineapple, peeled
- 2 cups of fresh spinach
- 1 stalk celery stalk

Instructions

1. Put the ingredients in the Magic Bullet blender in order, then close the lid.
2. Set the Magic Bullet blender to its slowest speed initially, then quickly raise it to its fastest setting.
3. Use the tamper to push the ingredients toward the blades, and blend for one minute or until the desired consistency is reached.

102. ZUCCHINI BLUEBERRY SMOOTHIE

Prep Time: 5 Minutes | Freezing Time: 24 Hour

Total Time: 24 Hour 5 Minutes | Serving: 2

Ingredients

- 1/4 tsp ground cinnamon
- 2/3 cup of sliced zucchini
- 1 large stem celery
- 1 cup of light coconut milk
- 1 handful of greens
- 1 tbsp hemp seeds
- 1 large ripe banana
- 1 cup of frozen wild blueberries
- 1/2 tsp maca powder (optional)

Instructions

1. Mix everything in a high-speed Magic Bullet blender on high until it is smooth and creamy. If you think the flavor is too strong, add more cinnamon, banana, or zucchini to make it taste creamier, warmer, or spicier.
2. Spread it out in two glasses (or more or less if you want to change the batch size), and if you wish, you can decorate it with blueberries and hemp seeds. Fresh is best. Cover leftovers and put them in the fridge for up to 24 hours.

103. STRAWBERRY FIG SMOOTHIE

Total Time: 10 Minutes | Serving: 4

Ingredients

- ½ cup of granola
- 3 cups of almond milk
- 2 cups of frozen strawberries
- 8 dried figs

Instructions

1. Put the ingredients in the Magic Bullet blender in order, then close the lid.
2. Set the Magic Bullet blender to its slowest speed initially, then quickly raise it to its fastest setting.
3. Blend for 45 seconds or until the consistency you want is reached.

104. CARROT GINGER TURMERIC SMOOTHIE

Total Time: 20 Minutes | Serving: 2

Ingredients

Carrot Juice:

- 2 cups of carrots
- 1 1/2 cups of filtered water

Smoothie:

- 1 large ripe banana
- 1 cup of frozen or fresh pineapple
- 1/2 tbsp fresh ginger
- 1/4 tsp ground turmeric
- 1/2 cup of carrot juice
- 1 tbsp lemon juice
- 1 cup of unsweetened almond milk

Instructions

1. Put filtered water and carrots in a high-speed magic bullet blender. Blend on high until the carrots are totally smooth and pureed. If it doesn't blend well, you may need to add more water or scrape down the sides.
2. To use the juice, put a big, thin dish towel over a mixing bowl and pour the juice over it. Next, lift the corners of the towel and start twisting and squeezing the juice out until all of it comes out. Put pulp aside for smoothies or baked goods, like carrot muffins.
3. Move the carrot juice to a mason jar. It will last for a few days, but it tastes best when it's still fresh.
4. Putting the smoothie ingredients into the blender and turning it on high will make it creamy and smooth. It won't blend well unless you add more carrot juice or almond milk. Clear the sides if you need to.
5. Depending on your taste, add more banana or pineapple for sweetness, lemon for sourness, ginger for spice, or turmeric for warmth.Divide between two glasses and serve.

105. STRAWBERRY MANGO SMOOTHIE

Total Time: 5 Minutes | Serving: 1

Ingredients

- 1 banana (room temperature)
- 1 cup of frozen strawberries
- ½ cup of ice
- 1 cup of frozen mango
- ¼ cup of Greek yogurt
- 1 cup of milk (or almond milk or oat milk)
- 1 tbsp fresh lemon juice

Instructions

1. Put everything into a Magic Bullet blender and break up the banana. Turn off the blender and scrape the sides as needed to make it creamy and frothy. You can decorate it with a frozen strawberry and a frozen mango if you want to. You can eat it right away or put it in a jar with a lid and put it in the fridge for one day.

106. BLUEBERRY SMOOTHIE

Total Time: 5 Minutes | Serving: 2

Ingredients

- 1 large ripe banana, broken into pieces
- ½ tsp cinnamon
- 2 tbsp to ¼ cup of water
- ½ cup of Greek yogurt
- 1 medium carrot
- 2 cups of frozen blueberries

Instructions

1. Cut the carrot into small pieces. Put the water and Greek yogurt in the bottom of the Magic Bullet blender. Next, add the banana, frozen blueberries, cinnamon, and carrot.
2. Blend on high until a smooth purple puree forms. If necessary, scrape the sides and add a little more water. Serve right away.

107. MANGO SMOOTHIE

Total Time: 5 Minutes | Serving: 2

Ingredients

- ½ cup of milk
- 1 tbsp fresh squeezed lemon juice
- 5 ice cubes
- 3 cups of frozen mango (or fresh)
- ½ cup of water
- 1/2 banana

Instructions

1. Using a magic bullet blender, add all the ingredients, starting with the liquids and then the other ingredients, except for 2 cups of frozen mango.
2. Make a smooth mixture.
3. Add the two cups of frozen mango and blend until smooth. Add a little additional water or milk to make the blending easier.

108. CHERRY BERRY BEET SMOOTHIE

Total Time: 5 Minutes | Serving: 1

Ingredients

- 1 Orange, Skin removed, cut in half
- ½ cup of Coconut Milk or Plain Yogurt
- 1 Very Small Beet, Washed, Ends cut off
- ½ cup of Frozen Strawberries
- 1 Banana, broken in half
- ¼ cup of Water or Coconut Water
- 1 tsp Vanilla
- ¼ cup of Frozen Cherries
- Honey or maple syrup, to taste (optional)

Instructions

1. In the order given, put all ingredients in a magic bullet blender (high speed is best). Leave out the honey.
2. Slowly turn up the speed until the mixture is completely smooth. This could take 1-2 minutes.
3. For more sweetness, taste it and add maple syrup or honey if you like. If you want to add sugar, bend again for about 10 seconds.

109. KALE AND PEAR GREEN SMOOTHIE

Total Time: 11 Minutes | Serving: 4.75

Ingredients

- 1 small banana, peeled
- 2 cups of ice cubes
- 1 medium orange, peeled, quartered
- ½ Bartlett pear, cored
- 1 cup of green grapes
- ½ cup of water
- 1 cup of kale

Instructions

1. Put the ingredients in the Magic Bullet container in the order given, and then close the lid.
2. Set the Magic Bullet blender to its slowest speed initially, then quickly raise it to its fastest setting.
3. Use the tamper to push the ingredients toward the blades, and blend for 45 seconds or until your desired consistency is reached.

110. MINTED BERRY SMOOTHIE

Total Time: 11 Minutes | Serving: 3

Ingredients

- 1 tsp vanilla extract
- 1 tbsp fresh mint leaves
- 2 cups of almond milk
- 2 tbsp dates
- 1 cup of kale
- 2 cups of frozen mixed berries
- 2 tbsp kiwis

Instructions

1. Put the ingredients in the Magic Bullet container in the order given, and then close the lid.
2. Set the Magic Bullet blender to its slowest speed initially, then quickly raise it to its fastest setting.
3. Using the tamper to push the ingredients toward the blades, blend for one minute or until the desired consistency is reached.

111. GLOWING GREEN SMOOTHIE

Total Time: 11 Minutes | Serving: 5

Ingredients

- 1 apple, cored, halved
- ½ lemon, peeled
- ¾ pound romaine lettuce
- 3 celery stalk
- 1 banana, peeled
- 1 pear, cored, halved
- 1½ cup of water
- 1½ cup of baby spinach

Instructions

1. Put the ingredients in the Magic Bullet blender in order, then close the lid.
2. Set the Magic Bullet blender to its slowest speed initially and quickly raise it to its fastest setting.
3. Use the tamper as needed to blend for 45 seconds or until smooth.

112. PEACH MANGO SMOOTHIE

Total Time: 5 Minutes | Serving: 2

Ingredients

- ¼ cup of Greek yogurt (or substitute non-dairy milk)
- ½ tsp vanilla extract
- 1 cup of frozen peach slices
- 1 banana (room temperature)
- ¼ cup of milk (or almond milk or oat milk)
- ½ cup of 100% orange juice (unsweetened)
- 1 cup of frozen mango chunks
- 6 ice cubes

Instructions

1. Put everything into a Magic Bullet blender and break up the banana. Turn off the blender and scrape the sides as needed to make it creamy and frothy. Add a frozen peach as a garnish if you want to. You can eat it right away or put it in a jar with a lid and put it in the fridge for two days.

113. BEET & POMEGRANATE SMOOTHIE

Total Time: 5 Minutes | Serving: 2

Ingredients

- ¼ cup of fresh, raw beets diced
- 1 tbsp honey or more to taste
- 1 cup of spinach
- ½ banana frozen
- 1 cup of unsweetened vanilla almond milk
- ¼ cup of fresh pomegranate seeds

Instructions

1. Put everything into the Magic Bullet blender.
2. Start with a low speed and slowly raise it to high for 60 to 90 seconds or until the mixture is smooth.
3. Pour and eat right away!

114. CARDAMOM CASHEW SMOOTHIE

Total Time: 5 Minutes | Serving: 2

Ingredients

- 1/4 tsp ground cardamom, more to taste
- 2 frozen bananas
- 4 medjool dates
- 1 cup of cashew milk (or other nut milk)
- 1 cup of ice
- 1/4 cup of cashews
- 1/2 tsp vanilla extract
- Pinch of cinnamon, optional
- Strawberries for garnish, optional

Instructions

1. Put everything into the magic bullet blender. Start with the liquid and add the ingredients in order of how soft and firm they are. To make this smoothie, put in layers of cashew milk, vanilla, cardamom, cinnamon (if using), dates, cashews, ice, and frozen bananas. Choose the smoothie setting that is already set up, or blend until all the ingredients are well mixed and the mixture is creamy. Cut it into two portions, and if you want, top each with a fresh strawberry.

115. PUMPKIN PIE SMOOTHIE

Total Time: 10 Minutes | Serving: 1

Ingredients

- 1/2 tsp ground cinnamon
- 1/2 cup of unsweetened almond milk
- 1/2 cup of pumpkin puree
- 1 frozen banana
- 1 tsp vanilla extract
- pinch each of nutmeg, ginger & allspice
- 1 tbsp almond or pecan butter
- ½ cup of plain or vanilla yogurt

Instructions

1. Put everything into a magic bullet blender and blend it until it's smooth.

116. SPIRULINA SMOOTHIE

Total Time: 5 Minutes | Serving: 1

Ingredients

- 1/2 cup of yogurt of choice
- 1/4–1/2 of an English cucumber
- 1–2 tsp of spirulina powder
- 1/2 cup of mango (or other frozen fruit)
- 1 banana or 1 cup of frozen cauliflower
- 1 cup of liquid
- 1 cup of chopped kale (or other greens)
- Optional for added sweetness: 1 Medjool date or 1/2-1 tbsp of maple syrup

Instructions

1. Put all the ingredients into a powerful magic bullet blender. Blend on high speed for one to two minutes or until the smoothie is smooth and there are no more chunks of kale.
2. Serve and enjoy!

117. SUNSHINE SMOOTHIE

Total Time: 5 Minutes | Serving: 1

Ingredients

- 1/2 cup of frozen cauliflower rice
- 1 tbsp acacia fibre
- f1.5 cups of almond milk
- 1 tbsp macadamia/coconut butter blend
- 1/4 zucchini
- 1 serving Equip Foods Vanilla Protein Powder
- 1 tbsp cacao powder

Instructions

1. Put all ingredients in a magic bullet blender and blend until smooth. After blending, add some chopped almonds and shredded coconut.

WEIGHT LOSS SMOOTHIE

118. ALMOND JOY BREAKFAST SMOOTHIE

Total Time: 5 Minutes | Serving: 1

Ingredients

- 1/4 zucchini
- 1.5 cups of almond milk
- 1 tbsp macadamia/coconut butter blend
- 1/2 cup of frozen cauliflower rice
- 1 tbsp acacia fibre
- 1 tbsp cacao powder
- 1 serving Equip Foods Vanilla Protein Powder (code JENNIFER)

Instructions

1. Put everything in a magic bullet blender and blend until smooth. After blending, add some chopped almonds and shredded coconut.

119. PEACH-RASPBERRY SURPRISE SMOOTHIE

Total Time: 15 Minutes | Serving: 3 ⅓

Ingredients

Peach-berry (bottom) layer:

- 1 tbsp hulled hemp seed
- ½ cup of frozen raspberries
- ½ cup of frozen peaches slightly thawed
- ⅓ cup of unsweetened almond milk or other non-dairy milk of choice
- ⅓ cup of peeled and chopped zucchini

Peach (top) layer:

- 1 tbsp hulled hemp seed
- ⅓ cup of unsweetened almond milk
- ⅓ cup of peeled and chopped zucchini
- 1 cup of frozen peaches slightly thawed
- Pinch of ground cinnamon, optional

Instructions

1. Put everything in a magic bullet blender and blend until smooth.
2. Split between two glasses. Use a flexible spatula to remove the puree, or rinse the magic bullet blender to make the layers stand out.
3. Add everything to magic bullet blender and blend until smooth. Spread the mixture between the two glasses and slowly pour the mixture down the side of each glass to keep the layers separate.
4. Put some frozen raspberries, hemp seeds, and zucchini slices on top to make it look nice.

120. PINEAPPLE WEIGHT LOSS SMOOTHIE

Total Time: 5 Minutes | Serving: 1

Ingredients

- Juice from 1/2 lime
- 1 tsp matcha green tea powder
- 1/2 banana, frozen (peel and freeze ahead of time)
- 1 tbsp coconut flakes (unsweetened, toasted works great too!)
- 3/4 cup of frozen pineapple
- 2 scoops collagen peptide powder
- 3/4 cup of unsweetened almond milk
- 3/4 cup of fresh spinach

Instructions

1. Put everything into a high-speed Magic Bullet blender and blend it until it is totally smooth.
2. Move to a glass and drink right away.

121. STRAWBERRY KIWI SMOOTHIE

Total Time: 5 Minutes | Serving: 2

Ingredients

- 1 cup of frozen strawberries
- ½ cup of almond milk
- ½ cup of Greek yogurt
- 1 tbsp honey
- 1 tsp vanilla extract
- 2 peeled, whole kiwis

Instructions

1. In a magic bullet blender, mix honey and almond milk. Vanilla extract, frozen strawberries, kiwi, and Greek yogurt should be on top.
2. Mix well. Put it in two glasses and enjoy!

122. SLIM GREEN SMOOTHIE

Total Time: 5 Minutes | Serving: 1

Ingredients

- ¼ cup of coconut water
- 1 tsp lemon juice
- 1 apple
- ¼ cup of orange juice, calcium-fortified
- 1-1/2 cups of spinach
- 1 cucumber1/4 cup of carrot juice
- 1 cup of diced pineapple

Instructions

1. Using a magic bullet blender, just put everything in and blend until smooth. After that, split it evenly into 4 servings and enjoy!

123. BLUEBERRY WEIGHT LOSS SMOOTHIE

Total Time: 5 Minutes | Serving: 1

Ingredients

- 1 tbsp almond butter (unsweetened)
- 1 scoop vanilla protein powder
- 200 ml almond milk (unsweetened)
- 1 small-to-medium-sized ripe banana (peeled)
- 1 handful of spinach (washed)
- 1 cup of frozen blueberries

Instructions

1. Put everything into a high-speed Magic Bullet blender and blend until it's smooth for two to three minutes.
2. Serve and enjoy!

124. PEANUT BUTTER BANANA SPINACH

Total Time: 3 Minutes | Serving: 1

Ingredients

- 1 banana sliced and frozen
- ½ cup of ice
- 1 cup of baby spinach
- ½ cup of almond milk
- 1 tbsp peanut butter
- 1 tbsp oats optional
- 2 scoops Vanilla Protein Powder optional

Instructions

1. Add the spinach smoothie ingredients to a magic bullet blender.
2. Blend until smooth. If it's too thin, add 1/8 of a cup of almond milk until you get the desired consistency.
3. After putting the smoothie into a glass, rinse the blender immediately so the ingredients don't stick to the inside.
4. Warm it up before serving.

125. KALE WEIGHT LOSS SMOOTHIE

Total Time: 5 Minutes | Serving: 1

Ingredients

- 1 cup of baby kale loosely packed
- 1 cup of frozen strawberries
- 1 tbsp almond butter
- 1 cup of frozen pineapple
- 1 banana peeled
- ¾ cup of unsweetened almond milk

Instructions

1. Put the frozen pineapple, kale leaves, banana, almond butter, and frozen strawberries in the high-speed Magic Bullet blender bowl in that order.
2. Mix until the mixture is creamy. If you need to, stop the blender and scrape down the sides. You can add more almond milk and blend it if the smoothie is too thick.
3. Put it in a glass and enjoy!

126. STRAWBERRY PINEAPPLE SMOOTHIE

Total Time: 5 Minutes | Serving: 1

Ingredients

- 1 tbsp almond butter
- 1 cup of frozen strawberries
- 1 cup of chopped fresh pineapple
- ¾ cup of chilled unsweetened almond milk, plus more if needed

Instructions

1. Mix the pineapple, strawberries, almond milk, and almond butter in a magic bullet blender. Add more almond milk if needed to get the consistency you want after processing until smooth. Serve right away.

127. CHIA SEED COCONUT & SPINACH SMOOTHIE

Total Time: 5 Minutes | Serving: 1

Ingredients

- 1 cup of spinach
- 1 scoop vanilla protein powder
- 2 tbsp of chia seeds
- 2 ice cubes
- 1 and 1/4 cups of coconut milk

Instructions

1. Put everything above into a magic bullet blender.
2. Blend until the mixture is smooth, like a smoothie.
3. Enjoy!

128. BERRY BLAST SMOOTHIE

Total Time: 10 Minutes | Serving: 5

Ingredients

- 1 1/2 cups of orange juice
- 1 tsp vanilla extract
- 1 cup of fresh or frozen strawberries sliced
- 3 cups of mixed frozen berries, raspberries, blueberries, and blackberries, thawed slightly
- 1 cup of light vanilla yogurt
- 1 tbsp sugar

Instructions

1. Put everything into a magic bullet blender. Put the lid on top and blend until everything is well mixed. Put it in glasses.
2. Leave out some of the juice if you want your smoothie to be thicker.

129. PINEAPPLE-GRAPEFRUIT DETOX SMOOTHIE

Total Time: 10 Minutes | Serving: 2

Ingredients

1. 1 small grapefruit, peeled and segmented, plus any juice squeezed from the membranes
2. 1 cup of ice
3. 1 cup of packed baby spinach
4. 1 cup of frozen diced pineapple
5. 1 cup of plain coconut water
6. ½ tsp grated fresh ginger

Instructions

1. Blend coconut water, pineapple, spinach, grapefruit, and any juices, ginger, and ice in a magic bullet blender. Blend or blend until smooth and foamy.

130. PEANUT BUTTER OATMEAL SMOOTHIE

Total Time: 5 Minutes | Serving: 1

Ingredients

- 1/4 cup of old-fashioned oats
- 1 tsp chia seeds, optional if desired
- 2 tbsp creamy peanut butter
- 1 whole banana
- 1/2 cup of soy milk

Instructions

1. Put everything into a magic bullet blender.
2. Blend the smoothie for 30 seconds or until it is smooth and creamy.
3. Put it in a glass, and if you want, top it off with banana slices and oats. You can eat it right away or put it in the fridge until you're ready.

131. CHOCOLATE SMOOTHIE

Total Time: 10 Minutes | Serving: 2

Ingredients

- 1 ½ tbsp unsweetened cocoa powder
- 1 tbsp peanut butter
- 2 very ripe bananas
- 6 ice cubes
- 1 cup of milk
- 1 tsp vanilla extract

Instructions

1. Put the peanut butter, pudding mix, cocoa powder, milk, ice cubes, and vanilla in a magic bullet blender. Blend on high speed until the mixture is smooth. Put into two glasses.

132. BERRY-MINT KEFIR SMOOTHIES

Total Time: 5 Minutes | Serving: 2

Ingredients

- 1 cup of frozen mixed berries
- 1 tbsp honey
- 1 cup of low-fat plain kefir
- 1-2 tbsp fresh mint
- ¼ cup of orange juice

Instructions

1. Mix kefir, berries, juice, mint leaves to taste, and honey in a magic bullet blender. Mix until smooth. (You can store the smoothies in the fridge for up to one day or the freezer for up to three months.)

133. BLUEBERRY BANANA CAULIFLOWER SMOOTHIE

Total Time: 5 Minutes | Serving: 1

Ingredients

- 1 cup of almond milk: you may need an extra 1/4 cup of or so to get the right consistency
- 1/2 frozen banana
- 1/2 cup of frozen blueberries
- 1/2 cup of frozen cauliflower rice
- 1 serving vanilla protein powder

Instructions

1. Put everything into a high-speed Magic Bullet blender.
2. Mix it up until it's creamy and smooth.
3. Pour the smoothie into a glass after it's been mixed.

134. APPLE KIWI GREEN SMOOTHIES

Total Time: 5 Minutes | Serving: 2

Ingredients

- 1 cup of unsweetened yogurt
- 1 banana, peeled
- 1 cup of water
- 3 kiwis, peeled and cubed
- 2 cups of spinach
- 1 large green apple, cored and chopped (keep the skins for extra fiber)

Instructions

1. Put the ingredients in the Magic Bullet blender in order and blend until smooth.

135. ORANGE CARROT SMOOTHIE

Total Time: 5 Minutes | Serving: 4

Ingredients

- 1 large carrot (peeled and roughly chopped)
- ¼ tsp turmeric
- 2-inch piece fresh ginger (thinly sliced)
- ice to taste
- ½ cup of water
- 1 large seedless orange (peeled)
- 1 medium banana
- 2 tbsp lemon juice
- 2 tbsp flax seed meal

Instructions

1. Put everything in a high-speed Magic Bullet blender and blend it until it's smooth. Add as much ice as you need to get the consistency you want.

136. CHOCOLATE BANANA SMOOTHIE

Total Time: 5 Minutes | Serving: 2

Ingredients

- 1 ½ tbsp maple syrup
- ⅓ cup of milk of choice
- ¼ cup of Greek yogurt
- 2 medium ripe bananas
- 1 ½ cups of ice
- ¼ cup of cocoa powder
- ½ tsp vanilla extract
- Optional: mix in 1 tbsp of peanut butter

Instructions

1. Put the ingredients in the Magic Bullet blender in the order given, making sure to break up the banana as you go. Stop and scrape down the sides of the bowl as needed, and add a little more liquid if needed. Blend until smooth and foamy. You can eat it right away or put it in a jar with a lid and put it in the fridge for two days.

137. PUMPKIN BANANA SMOOTHIE

Prep Time: 10 Minutes | Additional Time: 8 Hours 5 Minutes

Total Time: 8 Hours 10 Minutes | Serving: 2

Ingredients

- 1 banana, sliced
- 2 tbsp brown sugar
- 1 cup of pumpkin puree
- ¼ tsp vanilla extract
- 1 cup of milk
- ¼ tsp ground cinnamon

Instructions

1. Put pumpkin puree in a bag that can be closed again, and freeze for 8 hours overnight.
2. After taking the pumpkin out of the freezer, let it sit at room temperature for 5 to 10 minutes to soften.
3. Put pumpkin, banana, brown sugar, cinnamon, and vanilla extract into the magic bullet blender. Then add milk. Mix for about three minutes or until smooth.

138. PEACH COBBLER SMOOTHIE

Total Time: 5 Minutes | Serving: 1

Ingredients

- 1 tsp cinnamon
- 1 ½ cups of unsweetened vanilla almond milk
- ¾ cup of frozen peaches
- 3 ice cubes
- ½ cup of Quaker Old Fashioned Oats

Instructions

1. Put the above ingredients into a Magic Bullet blender in the order given. As long as it's smooth, blend for 45 seconds. Serve right away.

139. PINEAPPLE COCONUT SMOOTHIE

Total Time: 5 Minutes | Serving: 2

Ingredients

- 1/2 cup of pineapple juice
- 2 tbsp shredded, unsweetened coconut
- 1/2 cup of unsweetened coconut milk
- 1 tbsp honey
- 1/2 cup of yogurt vanilla
- 3 cups of frozen pineapple chunks, plus more for garnish

Instructions

1. Get the ingredients together.
2. Mix everything in a smoothie magic bullet blender. Mix until smooth.
3. Add pineapple chunks as a garnish. Serve right away.

140. BLUEBERRY SPINACH SMOOTHIE

Total Time: 2 Minutes | Serving: 1

Ingredients

- ¾ cup of unsweetened vanilla almond milk or milk of choice
- ½ tsp vanilla extract
- 1 large handful of baby spinach
- ½ cup of frozen blueberries
- 2-3 ice cubes
- 1 scoop vanilla protein, optional
- 1 tbsp almond butter, optional

Instructions

1. Put all ingredients into the Magic Bullet blender in the order given. Mix until it's smooth.

141. MANGO PEACH SMOOTHIE

Total Time: 5 Minutes | Serving: 2

Ingredients

- 1 cup of ice
- ½ tsp vanilla extract
- 1 cup of diced peaches, fresh or frozen
- 1 ½ cups of almond milk
- 1 cup of chopped mango, fresh or frozen

Instructions

1. Blend almond milk, peaches, mango, and vanilla in a Magic Bullet blender. Mix well.
2. Blend it some more after adding the ice until it's smooth. Add a little more almond milk if it's too thick.

142. COCONUT MILK SMOOTHIE

Total Time: 5 Minutes | Serving: 4

Ingredients

- 3 bananas
- 1 tsp vanilla extract
- ½ cup of ice
- 2 tbsp cashew or peanut butter
- 1 13-ounce can of coconut Milk
- ½ cup of unsweetened coconut flakes

Instructions

1. Add ice, cashew or peanut butter, bananas, coconut milk, vanilla, and coconut flakes to a Magic Bullet blender. Blend until smooth.
2. Mix well. Add some water to thin it out if it's too thick.

143. BLUEBERRY BEET SMOOTHIE

Total Time: 5 Minutes | Serving: 2

Ingredients

- 3/4 cup of frozen blueberries
- 1/2 cup of chopped or grated beets
- 1/2 banana
- 1 cup of milk of any kind

Toppings:

- more blueberries
- yogurt (plain regular or dairy-free)

Instructions

1. Mix all the ingredients in a magic bullet blender (except the toppings). Mix until smooth and creamy. If you need to, add more liquid.
2. Add anything that makes you happy on top. Enjoy!

144. BANANA SMOOTHIE

Total Time: 5 Minutes | Serving: 2

Ingredients

- 1 banana
- 1/4 cup of water or milk (dairy or non-dairy)
- 1/3 cup of Greek yogurt
- 1/2 orange, peeled and quartered
- 1 to 2 tsp honey, optional

Instructions

1. Cut the banana and orange into quarters, then put them in a blender. It can have yogurt and water (or milk) on top. Start the Magic Bullet blender and blend until it's smooth and creamy. After you taste it, add honey if you think it needs it.

145. STRAWBERRY PEACH SMOOTHIE

Total Time: 5 Minutes | Serving: 1

Ingredients

- 1/2 cup of frozen strawberries
- 1/2 cup of ice cubes
- 1/4 cup of fresh sliced banana
- 1/2 cup of frozen peaches
- 3/4 cup of orange juice
- 1/4 cup of plain, unsweetened Greek yogurt

Instructions

1. Use the magic bullet and put in ice cubes, strawberries, peaches, banana slices, yogurt, and orange juice.
2. After covering, process at a medium speed for fifteen to thirty seconds, using the tamper as needed. Spend 15 to 30 seconds on high speed until the smoothie is thick and smooth. Depending on the consistency you want, add more juice.
3. Serve the smoothie right away after pouring it into a tall glass.

146. CINNAMON ROLL SMOOTHIE

Total Time: 5 Minutes | Serving: 1

Ingredients

- ¼ cup of old-fashioned oats
- 1 cup of liquid (milk or water)
- ½ cup of yogurt of choice
- ½ tsp of cinnamon
- 1 tbsp maple syrup
- Frozen banana
- 1 scoop of vanilla protein powder
- ½ tsp of vanilla extract

Instructions

1. Put everything into a magic bullet blender and blend until it's smooth and creamy.
2. Enjoy!

147. ORANGE CREAMSICLE SMOOTHIE

Prep Time: 5 Minutes | Freezing Time: 3 Hour

Total Time: 3 Hour 5 Minutes | Serving: 2

Ingredients

- 1/2 cup of yogurt (vanilla or vanilla soy yogurt)
- 1 (11-ounce) can of mandarin oranges in juice
- 1/2 cup of pineapple (frozen chunks)
- 1 cup of soy milk (vanilla)
- 1 tbsp honey

Instructions

1. Gather the ingredients.
2. Open the orange can and drain the juice.
3. Put in a plastic bag with a zipper and freeze for a few hours.
4. Put the frozen pineapple and orange chunks in the bottom of a Vita-Mix or Magic Bullet blender.
5. Add the rest of the ingredients in the order given. Blend the ingredients until the texture of a milkshake is reached. If you want, you can add more ice until the mixture is freezing.
6. Serve and have fun!

148. PINEAPPLE PROTEIN GREEN SMOOTHIE

Total Time: 3 Minutes | Serving: 1

Ingredients

- 2 handfuls fresh spinach
- 1 cup of frozen pineapple chunks
- 1 scoop vanilla protein
- 1 cup of almond milk

Instructions

1. Put all ingredients into the Magic Bullet blender in the order given. Mix until it's smooth.

149. CARROT CAKE SMOOTHIE

Total Time: 5 Minutes | Serving: 1

Ingredients

- ½–1 cup of liquid (non-dairy milk and water)
- 1 large carrot, roughly chopped
- 2 pitted dates
- ½ of a frozen banana
- 1 tsp of cinnamon
- 8 walnuts
- Sprinkle of nutmeg, freshly grated is EXTRA delicious
- 1 tsp of vanilla
- Extra finely grated carrot for mixing in, optional

Instructions

1. In a high-speed Magic Bullet blender, blend all ingredients (except for the extra carrot) until the mixture is creamy and smooth.
2. If you want to, you can add more finely grated carrots (which is highly recommended!). After adding a few chopped walnuts, enjoy!

150. STRAWBERRY BLUEBERRY SMOOTHIE

Total Time: 5 Minutes | Serving: 2

Ingredients

- 1 banana (room temperature)
- 1/4 to 1/2 tsp cinnamon
- 1 tbsp maple syrup, honey, or agave syrup
- 1 cup of frozen blueberries
- 1 cup of milk (or almond milk or oat milk)
- 1 cup of frozen strawberries
- ¼ cup of Greek yogurt
- ½ cup of ice

Instructions

1. Put everything into a Magic Bullet blender and break up the banana. Turn off the blender and scrape the sides as needed to make it creamy and frothy. Add a strawberry and blueberries as a garnish if you want to. You can eat it right away or put it in a jar with a lid and put it in the fridge for one day.

Made in the USA
Middletown, DE
30 December 2024

68491694R00049